ALMOST

ESSENTIALS

Lyrics from my songs
Laurian Taler

GONG PUBLISHING
TORONTO

ALMOST ESSENTIALS
Lyrics from my songs

GONG PUBLISHING TORONTO
www.gongnog.com

ISBN 978-1-926477-00-8

Laurian Taler

Dedication

To all the lovers:
lovers of peace, lovers of harmony,
lovers of friendship, lovers of song, lovers of
poetry, and of course, lovers of love.

Especially to Minodora: my lover, my wife,
and mother of my children.

Foreword

My usual answer to the polite "How are
you?" is always "Almost Perfect!" which
tends to bring a smile here and there.
When I was to choose a title for my first book
of lyrics, "Essentials" alone wouldn't do,
especially since so much of everything is so
arguable, so I thought that adding "Almost"
might be an acceptable modifier to the
presumptuous title.
The poetry in this volume contains over one
hundred lyrics to an equal number of my
songs, some published in CD form, some
presented on my website called for good
reason www.gongnog.com.
Of course, the rhythm, the rhyme, the
cadence of the lyrics are all serving the songs,
as much as the songs are serving, together
with their words, the expression of the
emotions felt or imagined by me.
It is for you to decide if the lyrics are
provoking in you that lyrical reaction that
might be suggested, but a more complete
reaction would certainly come if you perused
them together with the music for which they

had been penned. If the question is put, what was first, the music or the lyrics, in my case it was always the music. In many instances, even before I wrote one line of lyrics, the title of the song was chosen and was directing me, because of the content of the music, to the content of the lyrics.

They describe what I would call situational relations, if this weren't a misnomer, because how can you have relations without situations, or situations without relations? Most of the songs are oozing with emotions derived from all the possible situations that can be encountered between lovers. In this sense, the title of the collection might be appropriate.

The first figures beside the lyrics title show the album or CD with the songs in the order in which songs had been created, the second figures show the track number in that grouping or album. At the end of the book you find a list of albums and their titles.

The book is the first volume in a series containing other lyrics, named "Songs of love and mores", to which volumes of poetry will be added. All the songs from this volume

could be found in mp3 format on a CD
especially created to be paired with the book.

In case you were wondering why is a wood sculpting
kit placed on the cover, some of the lyrics
on page 68 might deliver the poet's answer:

"Words are only tools we sculpt with
Into what some say is soul".

Table of Contents

Foreword   2
01 01. Fancy flower   8
01 02. If love comes like a wave   9
01 03 When you will come   10
01 04. You bring your happiness   11
01 05. Closer and closer   12
01 06. I love you so   13
01 07. Life's book   14
01 08. Dream enough   15
01 09. If you will come   16
01 10. All I wanted   17
01 11. You want to win   18
01 12. Try me   19
02 01. Come January   20
02 02. Amore is…   21
02 03. Be with me   22
02 04. What is happiness   23
02 05. Looking for trouble   24
02 06. Eyes longing   25
02 07. Children   26
02 08. Forbidden fiesta   27
02 09. Akiva's dream   28
02 10. Mambo blue   29
02 11. Who told you   30
02 12. Second try   31
03 01. Friday night   32
03 02. You are a boat   33
03 03. Tremor   34
0304. Harmonica time   35
03 05. Part of me   36
03 06. Kiss me gently   37
03 07. Pop Toselli   38
03 08. You swing your life   39

03 09. Enjoy		40
03 10. I wish I could		41
03 11. In thirty years		42
04 01. One rock too many		43
04 02. Simple love		45
04 03. Twist buddy		46
04 04. Forest walk		47
04 05. Einstein song		48
04 06. February blues		49
04 07. Come dance the samba		50
04 08. Bring me love my baby		51
04 09. One step mambo		52
04 10. Nothing new		53
05 01. Sunday sky		55
05 02. About happiness		56
05 03. I want to know		57
05 04. Wake up		58
05 05. Friendship		59
05 06. Hunger – hunger		60
05 07. Swing the night		61
05 08. Wonder		62
05 09. Find a way		63
05 10. Whatever you dig		64
06 01. Come and dance with me		65
06 02. Sing another song		67
06 03. A Poet's song		68
06 04. September Eleven		69
06 05. Days on		71
06 06. A slow foxtrot		72
06 07. Have hope		74
06 08. Conquer night		75
06 09. May ballad		76
06 10. Remember, baby, that I love you		77
07 01. A spring with sun		78
07 02. It happened		79
07 03. We go		80
07 04. Dance me		81
07 05. Relax		83
07 06. What do you know		84

07 07. There isn't another way   85
07 08. Tell me what's on your mind   86
07 09. Funny harmonica   87
07 10. Remember - remember   88
07 11. A dreamer   89
08 01. A rotten day   90
08 02. From a heart   91
08 03. Last encounter   92
08 04. Melancholy   93
08 05. Moves of passion   94
08 06. Into hot water   95
08 07. Share – share   96
08 08. Slow road   97
08 09. When coming through the crowd   98
08 10. The tale of Tristan and Isolde   99
09 01. Rega, Rega, Reggae   100
09 02. Trick me no more   101
09 03. Angry souls   102
09 04. Snow grass   103
09 05. We are burning rubber   104
09 06 Try a song   105
09 07. What you own   106
09 08. Good day to you   107
09 09. You gush fascination   108
09 10. What inspiration gives you   109
10 01. At the fest   110
10 02. Joy bossa nova   112
10 03. Man went out of jail   113
10 05. Only trouble   114
10 06. Remember what you said   115
10 07. Sing when sun   116
10 08. Songs are to sing   117
10 09. Schools start in Autumn   118
10 10. The meek inherit the Earth   119

List of Albums   120

01 01. **Fancy Flower**
Music and lyrics ©Laurian Taler, 1998
1
A fancy flower
Trembles timid in my heart
Its flutter hurts me
But I fancy it from start
It feels like fire
It brings desire
It brings the sweetest pain
Into my veins
2
This fancy flower
I will care with my heart
I'll keep it growing
And I'll make it turn just right
Its scent is heaven
Indeed is heaven
I can't compare it
With something else
Chorus (2x)
They call it love
And love it is
There is no other name
My blood will boil
Or it will freeze
And I am fair game
3 (2x)
A fancy flower
Trembles timid just for you
Its flutter hurts me
But I don't know what to do
I want to chase you
And to embrace you
I want to place you
Into my soul
Chorus (2x)

01 02. **If Love Comes Like A Wave**
Music and lyrics ©Laurian Taler, 1998

1
If love comes like a wave
I am an island
Battered by the rough sea
That shakes the soul in me
If love comes like a wave
I am an island
To which the sirens go
To sing my low

Chorus
I don't know why love is always
Everything for everyone
I don't know how love can power
All the deeds that have been done
What I know is that my being
Is enraptured with your seeing
As my deepest thoughts ring true
I'm aware that I love you
2
If love comes like a storm
I am a mountain
My top in fog is high
My forests hug the sky
If love comes like a storm
I am a mountain
The lightning strikes at me
So I can see
3
If love comes like a rain
I am a river
My waters boil and dart
Breaking all dams apart

If love comes like a rain
I am a river
I mighty overflow
To love and grow

01 03. **<u>When You Will Come To Me Again</u>**
Music and lyrics ©Laurian Taler, 1998

1
When you will come to me again
You'll find me waiting full of love
You'll know the softness of my strokes
You'll feel the sweetness of my kiss

2
When you will come to me again
My eyes will gaze in ecstasy
My heart will tremble like a string
'Cause so much happiness you bring
  Chorus 1 (2x)
And I will pirouette with you
And I will sing my songs with you
And I will stroke your lovely hair
And I will breath you with the air

  Chorus 2 (2x)
You'll be surprised of so much love
You'll be enchanted of my love
You'll sing and dance and love with me
And love, love me
And love, love me

01 04. <u>You Bring Your Happiness To Me</u>

Music and lyrics ©Laurian Taler, 1998

A1

You bring your happiness to me again, again
I am a draughty land that laughs
Under the rain
Your eyes catch mine and say so much
Your smile is better than a touch
You bring your happiness to me again, again

A2

You bring your happiness to me again, again
You make me know what really is the sweetest pain
I want your love and its return
For you and for your love I burn
You bring your happiness to me again, again

B1

So long ago
I thought it's no
That you may never
Never be mine
But you gave me
Your symphony
And so forever
For us it will be sunshine

B2

I want to bring
My soul to you
But my soul is shy
Just like a dove
I want to sing
My song to you
So that you know
The Music of my true love

B3

Your dawn embrace
Is my daily grace
And your caresses
Bring me your blesses
Your frenesy
Is my ecstasy
Your laughter always
Makes me know what's happiness

01 05. **<u>Closer And Closer</u>**
Music and lyrics ©Laurian Taler, 1998
A1
Closer and closer
When I dance with you
My eyes and your eyes
Make the world anew
I grow the longing
With you to belonging
Wave after wave
After you I crave
Bodies together
I wonder whether
Time disappeared
Like between us space

A2
Slower and slower
When with you I dance
Your body's softness
Brings me to a trance
I cannot tell you
How much I value
This moment's fullness
Mad in happiness
I cannot tell you
How much I value
This moment's fullness
Mad in happiness

B
In my arms with you my darling
Every sound's a symphony
In my arms with you my darling
We discover harmony

In my arms with you my darling
Every sound's a symphony
In my arms with you my darling
We discover harmony

01 06. **I Love You So**
Music and lyrics ©Laurian Taler, 1998

1
I love you so
I hardly know
Why such a fire
Scorches my heart
And why I hope a smile
From you part
The stars up glow
My heart is low
Alone in night
I love you so

  Chorus
I tried to tell you that I burn
Inside my soul just like a candle
To me you didn't want to turn
As for you, love was much to handle,
You went away, I followed you,
And so I will till I am through
2
I love you so
I hardly know
When time has come
And left me helpless
When my mind turns
My thoughts to that mess
The clock ticks dry
I eye the sky
My star is far
I love you so

01 07. **<u>Life's Book</u>**
Music and lyrics ©Laurian Taler, 1998
(INSPIRED BY A ROMANIAN BALLAD)

A
Leafing loosely through my life's book
I can see the ways that I took
Sometimes slowly in meanders
Swift in rapids full of wonders

Leafing loosely through my life's book
Can't recall the way that you look
As you burnt a hole in my heart
When you torn my life apart

B
But I don't understand
Why is your shadow on my mind
Why do you make me shake still
When to your face I'm blind

But I don't understand
What in that hole you left behind
Nobody filled it ever
With emotions of your kind

C
And when life's book I close
Oh sweet forgetfulness bring me peace
I think I'll rip the damn' book
This torture I won't miss

And when life's book I close
Oh sweet forgetfulness bring me peace
I think I'll rip the damn' book
This torture I won't miss

01 08. **Dream Enough**
Music and lyrics ©Laurian Taler, 1998
A1
Let's go back to our primal
State of innocence and mood
Let's go back to our childhood
When to wonder we still could

 CHORUS
'Cause childhood is a dream
And dreams are from the soul
We cannot dream enough
To get to our goal
'Cause childhood is a dream
And dreams are from the soul
We cannot dream enough
To get to our goal

A2
Let's imagine our wonders
Let's transform them into play
And become the equal players
In a new and better way

A3
Let's curb noises into Music
And turn shadows into light
Let's learn how to grow with nature
And to channel our might

A4
Let us conquer all the darkness
In the forest of mankind
Let us bring the light of loving
In the soul and in the mind

 CLOSING CHORUS
'Cause childhood is a dream
'Cause childhood is a dream
'Cause childhood is a dream
And dreams are from the soul
We cannot dream enough
We cannot dream enough
We cannot dream enough
To get to our goal

01 09.   **If You Will Come To Me Tomorrow**
Music and lyrics ©Laurian Taler, 1998

1
If you will come to me tomorrow
If you will come to me to stay
I will forget what's sorrow
I will go out my way
I will surround you with flowers
Be it December or May
2
If you will come to me tomorrow
If you will come to me to stay
I will forget what's sorrow
I will go out my way
I will surround you with flowers
Only to stay
  Chorus
And /(But) if you'll stay with me for ever
You will know what is happiness
And if you'll love me as I love you
We will spread our love to others
And our happiness
3
If you will come and go tomorrow
If you will shake your head and leave
You will lose me to sorrow
To pain you can't conceive
And you will also lose
Love of my heart

4
If you will come and go tomorrow
If you will shake your head and leave
I will have to grow in sorrow
Love to anyone I'll give
But you will also lose
Love of my heart

Laurian Taler

01 10. **All I Wanted In My Life**
Music and lyrics ©Laurian Taler, 1998

A
All I wanted in my life
Was to love you
And get your love

All I hoped was watch your looks
Enter my soul
And warm it up

Now that love is at an end
All I want is understand
Why I wanted all my life
So little I don't understand

B
As if love were all forever
As your love were life itself
I endured the pain of being
Just a toy on your play shelf

Now I know you used my tender
Love to satisfy your needs
I can no more be defender
Of your vile and empty deeds

A
All I wanted in my life
Was to love you
And get your love

All I hoped was watch your looks
Enter my soul
And warm it up

Now that love is at an end
All I want is understand
Why I wanted all my life
So little I don't understand

17

01 11. **You Want To Win**

Music and lyrics ©Laurian Taler, 1998

1
You want to be the best
To make a name
You always want to win
At any game
But winning is not all
As our mainly goal
Is to bring love yes love
To our souls

2
For money and for love
You always fight
No matter who is wrong
You think you're right
But life is compromise
To which you learn to rise
Until you turn so old
And maybe wise
Chorus
My desires wave in circles
Like the water in a pond
I'm the pond and my desires
Wave in me and way beyond

Tremors come and go to shatter
All my willingness to act
And my soul is changing colours
For ideals and for facts

01 12.   **Try Me**
Music and lyrics ©Laurian Taler, 1998

1
Try me just another time
Put on me another dime
Give me yet another chance
To love you

2
I do know that I was wrong
When I left you for so long
And I missed so many nights
To love you

  Chorus (2x)
Please my love
Don't reject me
I feel the same pain that you felt
When I left
3
I am now another man
I have changed and now I can
Stay with you for all my life
To love you

4
But if still you don't believe
That from now I will not leave
I will chain myself to you
To love you

  Chorus (2x)
Please my love
Don't reject me
I feel the same pain that you felt
When I left

02 01. **Come January**
Music and lyrics ©Laurian Taler, 1998, 2001

Come January I am going to have fun
This February I will go embrace the sun
I'll definitely hit in March the skiing slopes
In boat in April you might see me pull the ropes
May, June, July
I'll roam the sky
For August's sake
I'll take a brake

But in September I'll go back to school
And in October I will think so cool
While in November many things I'll man
Then in December the New Year I'll plan.

Viens janvier
Moi je vais très bien m'amuser,
En février
Je veux le soleil embracer,
En mars, eh bien,
Je vais faire prés du ski alpin,
Et en avril
Dans ma barque je vais faire des milles,
Mais, juin, juillet,
Je vole tout prêt,
Et juste en août
J'repause au goût....

Mais en septembre
J'retourne à l'école
Et en octobre
Je vais penser drôle,
Le mois d'novembre
J'apprends faire des plans
Et en Décembre
J'ébauche mon Nouvel An.

02 02. **Amore Is...**

Music and lyrics ©Laurian Taler, 1998

I am asking friends galore
What amore is
They are raising their shoulders
What amore is
I am getting most impatient
What amore is
Someone tell me by now

Amore is a Latin word, it says
Your heart is just filled with love
Your soul is embracing soul,
And you love
Amore is a Latin word, it says
You only survive with love
You only create with love
With endless love

As you go through life searching lovers
You will find some whispering soft
To your ears words like amore
Don't get lost, oh, don't get lost,
(da capo)

02 03. **Be With Me**
Music and lyrics ©Laurian Taler, 1998

1
What you have brought so fast
Into my life
A glance, a smile, a touch
And so much strife
You squeezed my arm
And made my face turn red
You pierced my eyes
And fancy things you said
You loved me with your might
A night

Chorus
All the other nights to follow
Were without you and were hollow
Of my pain you didn't care
Love you didn't want to share
Days were blank and nights were lonely
You left me with torture only
Suffering with all my might
For what we did that night

2
Since that night I want you
To be with me
Since that night always
Your eyes I can see
Since that night life
I don't know what it means
Since that night you
Became my distant prince
You've been my love all right
A night

Laurian Taler

Laurian Taler

02 04. **What Is Happiness**
Music and lyrics ©Laurian Taler, 1998

1
Many things they taught in classes
Even more they whipped our asses
What we learned was in the alleys
That life has mountains and valleys
2
We forgot to ask our questions
We forgot to build our bastions
We came out to fight our battles
But were driven more like cattle
R1
Now we know what is a river
Now we know why people shiver
But we still cannot deliver
What is happiness
R2
People wait for an anointed
While they let themselves exploited
Never finding, disappointed,
What is happiness
3
What they should teach now in classes
To empower all the masses
Is that life is to be cherished
And you fight for it till perished
4
Work makes you spring into action
Love will give you satisfaction
Treat yourself and others fair
And the crops of life you share
R3 (2x)
Build up friendships, conquer reason
Chase out evil, laugh a season
Be together, find your vision
That is happiness.

02 05. **Looking For Trouble**
Music and lyrics ©Laurian Taler, 1998

Looking for trouble, out in the streets
For trouble
Is what I call life, yeah,
Out in the dark streets for trouble
I am a cool bum, what do I care
Looking for trouble and a dime to spare

Someone gives, someone takes,
Someone steals, someone breaks,
Streets are cool, streets are cold,
I am angry, I get bold.

Life isn't roses, not for us bums
It isn't
Spare a quarter, man,
Maybe I can fill my stomach
Work disappeared, no one would care
Looking for trouble and a prick to share

I've got a fever, my feet are old
I'm stumbling
Spare a soul, man,
How am I to meet tomorrow
My eyes are circles, I have no glare
Punish the world, god,
They don't want to share

Looking for trouble, out in the streets
For trouble
We are so many, yeah
They know this and they are scared
What takes to clench fists
When you don't bare
Life is a fight, man,
Fight it if you dare.

02 06. **<u>Eyes Longing</u>**
Music and lyrics ©Laurian Taler, 1998

Whose eyes are longing
These eyes are longing
My eyes are longing
Are longing for you

Whose voice is trembling
This voice is trembling
My voice is trembling
When I'm calling you

Whose heart is pounding
This heart is pounding
My heart is pounding
A love beat that's true

Your eyes are
The stars that lead me
Your lips are
The fruits that feed me
Your smile is
The horn of plenty
Stealing my dreams

Your walk is
That of a goddess
Your talk is
So sweet and modest
Happiness you
Spread around you
It never dims.

02 07. **<u>Children</u>**
Music and lyrics ©Laurian Taler, 1998

Children
Children are the spice of life for
Children
Give you reasons for your hopes for
Children
Bliss in all hearts flower
Our lives empower
Are the fruits of love

Children
We expect them for so long as
Children
Make us always to belong for
Children
Shape our lives with meaning
Fill our lives with feeling
Children make us strong

As we love them, in time
Their love is so sublime
They fill our hearts ahoy
With pride and joy

As we love them in time
Their love is so sublime
In life they are what we all call
Our goal.

02 08.   **<u>Forbidden Fiesta</u>**
Music and lyrics ©Laurian Taler, 1998

What you do, you do today
Who has time to borrow
Do it well, and try again
Don't leave it for tomorrow

Write a poem, smell a rose,
Breathe in deep the air,
Hold your head proud in the crowd,
And play always fair

Know thyself and know your heart
And in due time test her
How else you'll know how to deal
The forbidden fiesta.

02 09. **Akiva's Dream**
Music and lyrics ©Laurian Taler, 1998

My elders said, "You be wise"
My mother said, "Early rise"
My father said, " You submit to the rulers"

My sister said, "Learn to mend"
My brother said, "Learn to bend"
My uncle said, "Count your friends and be funny"

My heart said, "Taste life in the full"
My brain said, "Do not be a fool"
My friends said, "Let us go downtown
And make money"

In a dream, like in life, you can hear much
But you cannot decide if you 're out of touch
You can turn, you can swirl from reality,
But the road your soul still must see

Take your dream, nurse it right
And will grow with might,
Make it be part of you, bring it out to light,
Live your dream, sing your dream
And will change you too
Life's only a song that rings true.

02 10 **Mambo Blue**
Music and lyrics ©Laurian Taler, 1998

Mambo blue for me and you
Mambo blue for Dave and Sue
Mambo blue the dancing is due
Come and have a great time

Mambo blue the band is on
Oh I ache to swirl and shake
Mambo blue the beat is so true

When we dance we change our mood
When we dance we feel so good
Mambo blue
Is hot and cool too

When we dance we change our mood
When we dance we feel so good
Mambo blue
Is hot and cool too

Put colour in your dancing
Mambo is life enhancing
Smile and shake while you're dancing
Mambo blue

Put colour in your dancing
Mambo is life enhancing
Put colour in your dancing
Mambo blue

02 11. **<u>Who Told You</u>**
Music and lyrics ©Laurian Taler, 1998

Who told you that I love you
It's a lie
I couldn't say I love you
If I die

The words are just too simple
The sounds are just too nimble
To tell of all that's going
In my heart

My lips are ever trembling
My mind goes blank when trying
To tell of all that's going
In my heart

Who told you that I love you
It's a lie
I couldn't say I love you
If I die
The words are just too simple
The sounds are just too nimble
To tell of all that's going
In my heart

My lips are ever trembling
My mind goes blank when trying
To tell of all that's going
In my heart

If I were a mighty painter
I would paint love every day
Love for you in all the colours
Love that words just
Cannot say
If I were a bird or singer
I would sing love every night
Love for you in all the birds' songs
Love that words just
Can't say right.

02 12. **<u>Second Try</u>**
Music and lyrics ©Laurian Taler, 1998

I am at a second try
I'm trying to reach the sky
Nobody will stop me now
For I know
I know much more
The second time

My spirit to heaven soars
Because now I know much more
I can make it just so far and so high
Now on my second try

I am proud I'm trying
What life is, what life is,
If you don't try
I am proud I 'm bragging,
But I want to try
Reach the sky
The second time.

03 01. **Friday Night**
Music and lyrics ©Laurian Taler, 2000

1
Friday night, change your shoes,
'Cause you love it,
Friday night, dress like cool,
 'Cause you love it,
Show discreet elegance,
Meet your friends, go to dance,
Friday night, Friday night,
Go to dance!
2
Seize the time, seize the place,
 'Cause you love it,
Step right in, at your pace,
 'Cause you love it,
Life's a choice, take a chance,
Bring out that radiance
Friday night, Friday night,
Go to dance!
And start a romance!

Chorus (2x)

Dance with glee, and dance with bliss
You swing in the rhythm
Smile around, and steal a kiss,
It's allowed
You swing in the rhythm
Wave your waist
Turn around
Feel the sound
You swing in the rhythm
Resonate
Undulate
Hug your mate
You swing in the rhythm
Now
It's romance!

03 02. **You Are A Boat**

Music & lyrics ©Laurian Taler, 2000

1
You are a boat
On the river of time
When you rock, when you float
You are always sublime

You are a boat
Rocking gently 'n my mind
Cross the river with me
I won't leave you behind

 Chorus
So many waves
So far the ports
Winds overwhelm
And so many other perils

So many waves
So far the ports
Winds overwhelm
But I steady hold the helm

2
You are a boat
I am floating with you
It's the waltz of our life
Be it river or strife

You are a boat
I'm transported with you
I'm transfigured by you
I'm your sea, I'm your blue

Almost Essentials

Chorus

03 03. **Tremor**
Music & lyrics ©Laurian Taler, 2000

What kind of tremor
Fancy tremor
Passes my heart

What kind of tremor
Fancy tremor
Echoes my soul

It is the tremor
Fancy tremor
That you, love mine
Provoke, create and swirl
Just with your presence

Tremor, tremor
Are you so divine
Tremor, tremor
Comes from you
Love mine

Tremor, tremor
Fill another cup
Tremor, tremor
How you lift me up

Tremor again (10x)

03 04. **<u>Harmonica Time</u>**
Music and lyrics ©Laurian Taler, 2000

Play the harmonica now for my soul
It brings back memories I can't control
It brings back feelings of another time
A time that wasn't just another time
Harmonica, bring back that other time

Time for joy and time for laughter
Time for pearl drops on my face
Time for hope and morning after
Time for life at other pace

Time to gaze at you forever
Time to hold you in my arms
Time to watch your stars and never
Never quench off from your charms

03 05. **Part Of Me**
Music and lyrics ©Laurian Taler, 2000

Part of me has gone to heaven
Part of me has gone to devil
Part of me has gone away
Where you have wanted me to stay

Part of me has gone in hiding
Part of me has gone in sliding
Part of me has gone away
Where you have wanted me to stay

Chorus
If you wanted me again
Be it sunny, snow or rain
You will have to get my soul
Or you'll have to get me whole

03 06. **Kiss Me Gently**
Music and lyrics ©Laurian Taler, 2000

1 (2x)
When you'll come to me
Tonight to give me love
You will know how I want
You to reach for me

Chorus

Kiss me gently
Kiss me gently
Kiss me gently
Kiss me gently
 Kiss me gently
Kiss me gently
Tonight,
Tonight / My love

2
How I long for this encounter
How I long for you tonight
Hurry now, I can't be patient
Knowing how you'll reach for me

03 07. **Pop Toselli**
Music and lyrics ©Laurian Taler, 2000

1
What Toselli sang for us
Put me always in a trance
Put me always in a trance

What I do with it
Is what I think he'd liked
Put Toselli back to dance
Put Toselli back to dance

2
What a dream, a wonder dream
I am holding you 'n my arms
So ecstatic of your charms

And you share with me
The beauty of this song
As Toselli would have liked
I'm so sure
As Toselli would have liked

Chorus (2x)

Love is always
Under my eyes
Love is always
Under your eyes
 Love fills our hearts
With magic
Happiness
Happiness

03 08. **You Swing Your Life**
Music and lyrics ©Laurian Taler, 2000

You swing your life
You swing your life
And dearest hopes
Around the net of ropes
On to a higher branch

Aiming the top
You feel some kind
Of dizziness
The dizziness that some
Would blindly
Call success

Yet up no more
And down no more
Is life as known
The branch is thin
The fight is mean
It's for a bone

You win to lose
A false excuse
To reach the top
Your eyes you raise
Higher to hop
But lose your base

03 09. **Enjoy**
Music & lyrics @Laurian Taler, 2000

Enjoy the good times
Every moment
Enjoy the good times
Every day
Enjoy the good times
Every moment
And build your happiness
In every way

Forget the bad times
Seize the moment
Forget the bad times
Seize the day
Forget the bad times
Seize the moment
And build your happiness
In every way

2
Sometimes things or someone
Spoil your mood, your good time
Sometimes you alone
Are sad to the bone

1b
Forget the quarrel
Have a good time now
Forget the quarrel
Come dance with me
Forget the quarrel
Have a good time now
The dance will make you feel
In harmony

3 (2x)
Your life is only yours to make
Your time is only yours to take
You may treat your life as a toy
Or you treat life full to enjoy

03 10. **I Wish I Could**
Music & lyrics ©Laurian Taler, 2000

1 (2x)
I wish I could turn back the time
To when father held me on his neck
I wish I could turn back the time
So that I could give him what he'd missed

2 (2x)
A walk to park, a play with stones
And a little song, a throw of cones
A secret handshake, two kind words
So that I could give him what he'd missed

3
War just took him
Like a tree leaf
And then dropped him
In its whirl
Lands and people
Kept him long time
As an oyster keeps its pearl
And he suffered in his slavery
And we suffered 'cause his bravery
When he came back
I was too old to be carried
On his back
I forgot the games he taught me
And he had to find his track

2 (2x)
A walk to park, a play with stones
And a little song, a throw of cones
A secret handshake, two kind words
So that I could give him what he'd missed

1 (2x)
I wish I could turn back the time
To when father held me on his neck
I wish I could turn back the time
So that I could give him what he'd missed

03 11. **In Thirty Years**
Music and lyrics ©Laurian Taler, 2000

In thirty years
What you gave us was bliss
In thirty years
A caress and a kiss
And all the soul
That you put in our lives
You made the goal
Of a parent so wise

In thirty years
Dreams have grown into life
In thirty years
You became someone's wife
You danced your swings
And amassed your awards
You sounded chords
Which have fluttered gold wings

And now you make
Most people cry
Watching your shows
They beautify
Their own life
Their own strife
And then they glow
Like other suns and stars

In thirty years....

04 01. **One Rock Too Many**
music and lyrics ©Laurian Taler, 2000

1
One rock too many
Creeps now in my life
One rock too many
Cuts in like a knife
One rock too many
One rock too many
One rock too many
Creeps now in my life

One rock too many
Gives me a bad taste
One rock too many
And my time's a waste
One rock too many
One rock too many
One rock too many
Gives me a bad taste

2
Trying to get rid of it
I sing something else
Trying to get rid of it
I dance something else
But it keeps coming
But it keeps coming
The rock keeps coming
Coming back to me

Trying to get rid of it
I sing something else
Trying to get rid of it

I play something else
But it keeps coming
Yeah, it keeps coming
The rock keeps coming
Coming back to me

3 (a, b)
I cannot keep it out at all of my mad mind
I cannot keep it out at all of my mad mind
It is the beat the beat the beat that grinds
It is the beat that nowhere else I cannot find
Nowhere
I cannot keep it out at all of my mad mind
I cannot keep it out at all of my mad mind
It is the beat the beat the beat that grinds
It is the beat that nowhere else I cannot find
Nowhere
Nowhere
Nowhere
Nowhere
(a) Nowhere

(b) Nowhere else

04 02. **<u>Simple Love</u>**
Music and lyrics ©Laurian Taler, 2000

A1
What I want is simple, simple
Just simple love
What I want is simple, simple
Just simple love
I don't want no prince and horse
I don't want no dough or force
Give me simple, simple love
Give me simple, simple love
Give me simple, simple love

A2
What I want is candid, modest
Innocent love
What I want is simple, simple
Just simple love
I don't want no gold and pearls
I don't want no dukes or earls
Give me simple, simple love
Give me simple, simple love
Give me simple, simple love
B1
Come, come and laugh and cry with me
Come and play and dream with me
What is life if not
All the love we've got
Come and love and live with me
B2
Come, come and grow and work with me
Come and play and dream with me
What is life if not
All the love we've got
Come let's share our simple love

04 03. **Twist Buddy**
Music and lyrics ©Laurian Taler, 1999

1
Twist, buddy, twist, buddy
Twist what you have
Twist and then rev
Twist what you have

Twist buddy, your body
Twist while you can
Like in Milan
And like in Vatican

2
Twist like a priest around its flock
Twist like a handle round-the clock
Twist like a dancer at a feast
You do your twist
You do your twist

Twist like a beast around its tail
Twist like a rope around a sail
Twist like you are the best artiste
You do your twist
You do your twist

3
With your legs of rubber
Twist from evening until dawn
With your hips you clobber
Everyone that is a yawn
With your arms you pummel
With your fists you pummel
Better than a camel
Whoever's a yawn.

04 04. **Forest Walk**
Music and lyrics ©Laurian Taler, 1999

A1
We walk through the thick of autumn leaves
We gaze at the colours of the woods
With eyes full of light
With hearts full of dreams
We gather enchantment

A2
So we walk through life like all the leaves
We grow and we green like all the leaves
But sun doesn't fail
To burn and to pale
The torments of our lives

B1
What comes after all the leaves have gone
What comes after all the light has gone
What comes after all the life has gone
What comes then after
Nobody knows

But

B2
Light comes always out another spring
Leaves break out on trees another spring
Life springs everywhere another spring
That's what comes always after all

04 05. **Einstein**
Music and lyrics ©Laurian Taler, 2000

Intro
I shall tell you a story
Story of stars and stone
I shall tell you a story
Story of flesh and bone
Nobody told this story
Just so in song and verse
Of man and stone's the story
Of man and Universe
This story is of stars and stone
Stone bright and ever full of thought
Thought that has let us fly in space
Space that is bending over time
Time that is shorter than its rhyme
Rhyme that is a paradigm
Rhyme that is a paradigm

A
Once
There was a stone
Oh, and what a stone
Stone just full of might
Stone just full of light
Great wisdom stone
Kind, honest stone

B
This stone was a mensch (4x)
Great wisdom stone
Kind, honest stone
And this stone the folks knew by his strange name
Einstein

C
Einstein brought us might
Einstein brought us light
Einstein bent the space
Einstein timed the pace
Matter's energy
When speed of light
Squares all so bright

04 06. **February Blues**
Music and lyrics ©Laurian Taler, 2000

A1
It's time for a slow
A slow dance with you
You, my love
My love, only you
You 're close to my heart
Heart, my love

A2
My time is your time
Our steps flow in rhyme
Two hearts sing
Our eyes are ablaze
With each other's glaze
Worshiping

B
Only you, only you, only you
Keep me so close to you, close to you
I feel all that's to feel
What can I give you, love mine
Nothing else but love

What can I give you, love mine
Nothing else but love

A3
The day's getting long,
The cold's getting cruel
It's not March
I hold you and dance
It is our trance
Blues and all

A4
It's time for a slow
A slow dance with you
You, my love
My love, only you
You 're close to my heart
Heart, my love

04 07. **Come Dance The Samba**
Music and lyrics ©Laurian Taler, 2000

A1
This samba is for dancing
This samba is for prancing
This samba is the spirit
Is the soul of our dance

A2
It's samba what we cherish
We dance it till we perish
It's samba yes, it's samba
That keeps flowing in our veins

B1 (2x)
Come dance the samba and enjoy it now
Come dance the samba, I will show you how
This lovely rhythm is right, it's for your taste
Come wave your limbs and wave your waist

04 08. **Bring Me Love My Baby**
Music and lyrics ©Laurian Taler, 1999

A1
Bring me love my baby
Bring me love my baby
Bring me all the love you can
Bring me love my baby
Bring me love my baby
Bring me as I am your man

A2
Bring me love my baby
Bring me love my baby
How long do you think I'll wait
Bring me love my baby
Bring me love my baby
I will go to meet my fate

B
Bring me love my baby
Bring me love my baby
Bring me all the love you can
Bring me love my baby
Bring me love my baby
Bring me all the love you can

Life gushes with many dangers
Love's the only bliss
I don't want to mess with strangers
Just your love I'll miss

04 09. **One Step Mambo**
Music and lyrics ©Laurian Taler, 2000

A1
One step - mambo
Two step - mambo
This is the mambo-dance
Three step - mambo
Four step - mambo
This is the mambo-dance
Five step mambo
Six step mambo
This is the mambo-dance
Seven step mambo
Eight step mambo
This is the mambo-dance

bis

B1
Dancing mambo can inspire
Poems, songs, and love
Dancing mambo can inspire
Much more than above

B2
Dancing mambo can inspire
Me to dance with you
Dancing mambo can inspire
Something "entre nous"

04 10. **<u>Nothing New</u>**
Music and lyrics ©Laurian Taler, 2000

A1
Nothing new, nothing new
Under the sun
Nothing new, nothing new
And no fun
What is new
Doesn't count
What is old
Is just rant
Nothing new, nothing new
Under the sun

B1
Since I met you
Nothing counts more
Since I met you
World has stopped
Since I met you
Stars and see shores
Are just as far
As you are

A2
Nothing new, nothing new
For a change
Nothing new, nothing new
Feels now strange
Everything
Seems so staid
Everything
Seems to fade
Even my beautiful
Serenade

B1

A3
What is new, what is new,
I'm in love
What is new,
Doesn't come
From above
It's the burn in my chest
It's the mighty tempest
What is new, what is new
I'm in love

B2
Since I met you
I can't hear
Since I met you
I can't see
What I can do
Is to fear
That you might not
Be for me

05 01. **Sunday Sky**
Music and lyrics ©Laurian Taler, 2000

A

I'm under a Sunday sky
And so many stars are high
Where is my leading star
My star
So far

B1
My star is in heaven
Heaven number seven
I can't reach that level
That star is a devil

B2
My star's in my bowels
My star's in my vowels
My star is empiric
My star's in my lyric
Sky

...of my star

05 02. **About Happiness**
Music & lyrics ©Laurian Taler, 2000

I can't but wonder, wonder hard
About what?
About happiness (About happiness)
(bis)

When you try too hard to come so close
That you think you'll catch it now
It flies away and stays away from you
It is still
No more

2
Cause with happiness
And with lovingness
We fight loneliness
We fight idleness
We show wilfulness
We show eagerness
For it
For it
(bis)

3
We go climb
On every mountain
We go search
In every fountain
And we probe
With our love life
Happiness

We go climb
On every mountain
We go search
In every fountain
And we probe
And we probe
Happiness
(bis)

05 03. **I Want To Know**
Music and lyrics ©Laurian Taler, 2000

1
I want to know
Want to know who you are
I want to know
Want to know what you are
I want to know
Want to know why you are
Why in my mind
I' ve no answers to find

2

I want to know
Want to know how you feel
I want to know
Want your soul to reveal
How come your eyes
Warm my heart, warm my soul
How come your smile
Is for me so genteel

Chorus (2x)

And as you smile
Heavens are bright
And as you laugh
I cannot fight
The wave of love
That so much floods
My cup of love

05 04. **Wake Up**

Music & lyrics ©Laurian Taler, 2000

A
Wake up 'cause
Dreams are running nowhere
Dreams are running a - nowhere
You ought to
Wake for action, act out, dreamer
Time goes by if you don't simmer
(bis)
Dreams are running only if you act

B
Go out find your way around
Go and make it with your sound
Go and claim your right to be
As you have dreamed

Do your best and try again
Don 't be sleepy, don't be vain,
Serve your sisters, build a place,
Be full of grace

Count the seconds doing good
Waste no time in a bad mood
Live the present, face the future
Wake up!

05 05. **Friendship**
Music & lyrics ©Laurian Taler, 2000

A1
You call me friend
I call you friend
We are both liars
What's between us
So much fracas
Is something else
 (bis)

A2
You put me down
I put you down
We are both downers
To go like this
Doesn't make sense
For none of us at all

B
But,
Friendship
Whatever its name
Is what we want
Friendship
With all its meaning
Is what we want
Friendship
Be fight or quarrel
Is what we want
As when we
Were children
And truly friends
(bis)

05 06. **Hunger, Hunger**
Music & lyrics ©Laurian Taler, 2000

A
Hunger, hunger
Nobody can cheat it
Hunger, hunger
How can we defeat it
You are hungry
I am hungry
We are hungry
For too much
(bis)

B1
When we are hungry animals
We lose ourselves to hunger all
We lose our reason
We fall for treason
When we are hungry animals

B2
The satiated don't believe
The hungry ones, who may up-heave,
Some have it glutting
Yet some have nothing
It's sharing what we must achieve

05 07. **Swing The Night**
Music & lyrics ©Laurian Taler, 2000

A1
Swing the night again with all your passion
Swing the night again with all your might
Swing the night again, it is the fashion
Swing, swing the night
Swing it again

A2
Swing with all the stars bright up in heaven
Swing under the beams of a pale moon
Swing until the clock hits hour seven
Swing, swing the night
Swing in the tune

B
Holding you
Makes the swing
Such a great wonder
Holding you
Makes my heart
Swing so sweetly too
(bis)

C
You in my arms
You in my heart
Your smile makes wonders
You have the stars
Swing in your eyes
To cherish my soul

05 08. **Wonder**
Music & lyrics ©Laurian Taler, 2000

A1
Can I send my wave of wonder
Can I send my wave of wonder
Far in space
There where light and darkness
There where light and darkness
Hold their race
Time is running through my fingers
Time is running through my fingers
What I spend
Why the wonder, time and sparkle
Why the wonder, time and sparkle
So soon will end

B
I wonder why
And also
Why is a sky,
Why the sky is blue
And also
Why the day is through

or

I wonder why
Why is a sky,
Why it is blue
It isn't true

05 09. **Find A Way**
Music & lyrics ©Laurian Taler, 2000

A!
What do you want I cannot give
What do you give I do not want
What do you leave I cannot take
What do you take I cannot leave

A2
What do you love I also love
What do you hate I also hate
What do you want I cannot give
 What do you give I can't retrieve

B1
I try to find a way to answer
Why am I so confused and dry
I try to find a way to answer
Why do I wave from low to high

A1, A2

B2
I try to find a way to answer
Why do I feel a lonely mess
I try to find a way to answer
Why do you look for my caress

A1

05 10. **<u>Whatever You Dig</u>**
Music & lyrics ©Laurian Taler, 2001

A1
Whatever you dig
Dig so deep
Whatever you dig
Dig to find your gem
Whatever you dig
Dig so deep you reach
That what you search
In your life

B
Don't complain the granite
Is much too hard to riddle
Don't cry that the mud is
Not very fit to fiddle
Cling to your dig steadfast and
Hold your ground
Chase your hunt like a hound
Without a bound
(bis all)

A2
Whatever you dig
Dig so high
Whatever you dig
Don't lose sight of sky
Whatever you dig
Dig the dirt so clean
Soil will turn out
Without sin

A3
Whatever you dig
Dig in night
Whatever you dig
Dig to spread the light
Whatever you dig
Dig to bring in sun
Ditch out your find
For mankind

06 01. **Come And Dance With Me**
Music and lyrics ©Laurian Taler, 2004

A1
Come and dance with me
I'll kiss you with all my heart
Come and dance with me
Don't be afraid of love

My wish is to gaze rapt at your eyes
My wish is to warm up at your heart
My wish is to make you
Happier than dreams
(bis)

B
Life isn't long enough to linger
Life falls on you right from above
Make your choice, shine up your days
Make your choice forever love
Come dance with me right now
As the song invites

C
Come and dance with me
Be happy now
I care for you, I'll tell you how
Come and dance with me
Be happy now
Everything is hope for you and me

A2

The music calls you
To shake with glee your hips now
The music calls you
To hum and hum again

As your smile ignites a flame in me
Your shakes are so full of nobil'ty
And your grace is all
It is all just for love
(bis)

06 01. **Viens Et Danses Avec Moi (Come And Dance With Me)**
Music & lyrics ©Laurian Taler, 2001

A1
Viens et danses avec moi,
Je t'embrasse, mon coeur,
Viens et danses avec moi,
N'as pas aucun peur
(bis)
Ma foi c'est te garder dans les yeux,
Ma foi c'est la chaleur de ton feux,
Ma foi c'est te faire
 Heureux (se), heureux (se), heureux (se)
(bis)

B
La vie n'est pas longue pour attendre
La vie n'attends ceux qui esitent
Juste fais ton choix et brilles tes jours,
Juste fais ton choix pour ton amour
(bis)

C (instrum)

A2
La musique t'invite
À bouger tes hanches
La musique t'invite
À la fredoner
(bis)
Ton (Mon) sourire allume le feux en moi (toi)
Tes (Mes) mouvements - d'une reine pour son roi
Et ta (ma) grace est toute,
Toute pour t'aimer
(bis)

06 02. **Sing Another Song**
Music & lyrics ©Laurian Taler, 2001

A1
Sing another song with me
You know another song
Sing another song for me
You know another song
You can't forget
 Do not take me wrong
I need, I need your love much more
More than you brought me
Is that all you can give me now? (2x)

B1
Bring another way for me
You know another way
Bring another dream for me
You know another dream
 Do not take me wrong
I need, I need your love much more
More than you brought me yet
Do not take me wrong
Change your song

A2
With your voice
You can move the mountains
With your songs
You can melt the sky
Birds stop their flying
When they hear you sing
Bring me your love
 Quietly or sing

B2
With your voice
You can pass the oceans
With your songs
You can quench the thirst
Kids clear their voices
When they hear you sing
Bring me your love
Quietly or sing

06 03. **A Poets' Song**
Music & lyrics © Laurian Taler, 2001

A
Words are only tools we sculpt with
Into what some say is soul
Robbing and disrobing whole
What is sadness or is bliss

Sounds of thoughts we craft to see
Into lines of song and pain
Trying to make sense in vain
Of what life is or should be

B
Proud words we spread down
To chant and enchant - (as poets)
Humble we hope that
We write what we meant - (as poets)

Strings of our feelings
We try soft to twinge
Playing with words means
We sing and we singe

06 04. **September Eleven**
Music & lyrics ©Laurian Taler, 2001

Chorus A
September eleven
Everything changed
September eleven
Nothing has changed

Chorus B
September eleven
Everything changed

A1
World was turning
In its orbit
Like was always turning
When steel birds driven by hatred
On people collapsed
How much hatred
Drives a conscience
To change man in rabid devil
Hoping for a place in heaven
With a ghost as maid

Chorus B

A2
World still turns now
In its orbit
Like was always turning
But a heavy fog of hatred
On people descends
Life is fear
Life is dear
Life is no more than a tear

Life is no more than a mere
Number or pretence

Chorus B

B1
Faith is a death tool
Death is a first rule
Life is perverted,
Ah, all is hate
No god's a killer
Just men are dealers
Shorting with promise
To after date

Chorus A

B2 (instrumental)

Chorus A

B3
We breathe the air
Bombs in the air
Spores are floating in the air
Nothing, nothing changed
We breathe the air
Bombs in the air
Spores are floating in the air
Nothing, nothing changed

Chorus A, A2
Chorus A, A2
Chorus A

06 05. **Days On**
Music & lyrics ©Laurian Taler, 2001

A1
Days on and on, nights on and on go by,
Go by, go by
We go with them, we run with them while work,
While smile or sigh
We dream for morrow and another time
We knit the verses with another rhyme
We greet the sunrise and we fall in love
Again.

A2
Days on and on, years on and on we build
A nest for dreams
It doesn't matter if the rain or snow
Falls on its beams
We look around for our inner space
We sew in it the patterns of our lace
We draw the plans for yet another race
Again.

B1
All the many movements on this planet
Be it wind or water or the hail
Cannot stop our run
Cannot stop our fun
Cannot stop our manning of the sail.

B2
All the many-upheavals on this planet
Be it draught or riot or a war
Cannot stop our dreams
Cannot tear our seams
Cannot change us in our human core.

06 06. **A Slow Foxtrot**
Music & lyrics ©Laurian Taler, 2001

A1
We dance a slow foxtrot
Like the foxtrot
That we danced
First time we met
The beat of my heart thumps
Like the heart beat
That I felt
First time we met.

A2
We dance a slow foxtrot
While embracing
With our bodies
All our past
The past that we started
With a heart beat
And a glance
First time we met.

B1
We were thirsty for each other
We were begging for each other
We were crazy for each other
As soon as we touched

B2
We were hungry for each other
We were dashing for each other
We were dazzled by each other
As soon as we touched

B1 B2   B1 B2

A3
The dance is now slower
As we also
Are much slower
Than we were
But my love is truer
And more tender
Than it was
First time we met

C1
Taken by the waves of the song
We are gliding just as one whole
Taken by the waves of the song
We are feeling love in our souls

C2
It is our dance, our life
All the music and all the darn beat
What is lovely is that again we feel
As if it's the first time we meet.

06 07. **Have Hope**
Music & lyrics ©Laurian Taler, 2000

A1
Have hope
 Life is full when you hope
Have hope
If you hope then you cope
Have hope
You get strong when you do
And the sky gets rosy suddenly from blue
(2x)

B
Day to day hoping
That's what life is
Act upon your hopes and wonder
How you feel the fizz
Day to day hoping
That's what life is
Desperation will be vanquished
And you'll be at ease

A2
Have hope
Even down on a slope
Have hope
You will find there is scope
Have hope
You get strong when you do
You will always be a part of someone's crew
(2x)

B, A1, A2

06 08. **<u>Conquer Night</u>**
Music & lyrics ©Laurian Taler, 2000

A
Conquer night
Conquer night
It's your right
To reach the abyss
Conquer night
Conquer night
It's your right
To spread the light
What is dark without the light
What is day without the night
Conquer night
Conquer night
It's your right
To strike your light
It's your right
To strike your light

B
Light is knowing and
Is living what is truth
Night is living just by
What is nail and tooth
This is why you need to stand
With all your might
Strike your light
And conquer night
(Bis)

06 09. **May Ballad**

Music & lyrics © Laurian Taler, 2001

A
Around me everything is green
Blue sky and flowers can be seen
But dark ash is spread through my heart
As I have quarrelled with sweetheart

B
She didn't give me any chance
When with all my exuberance
I told her that I'll learn to fly
A one-man rocket cannon launched
To bring her stars from sky
To bring her stars from sky.

C
What should I do now, man?
She ' ll never let me go fly
What a circus made she
Saying that I'm a fall guy

06 10. **Remember, Baby**
Music & lyrics ©Laurian Taler, 2006

A
Remember, baby, that I love you
Remember, baby, that I love you
There is nothing else that needs now to be said
There is nothing else that you need to feel true
If you can remember all the nights and all the days
That we filled with hot love, with real love,
Going both ways
Then you can forgive me one more time

B
Remember, baby, that I love you
Remember, baby, that I love you, oh, so much
Our history together
Is a seal that we cannot break
We will stay happy together
With our love, with our love, with our love

C
People make mistakes 'cause they love and forget
People make mistakes when so heavy they bet
If one lets oneself caught in a pool of sin for a while
Then it's easy to end without love
B
Remember, baby, that I love you
Remember, baby, that I love you, oh, so much
Our history together
Is a seal that we cannot break
We will stay happy together
With our love, with our love, with our love

07 01. **A Spring With Sun**
Music and lyrics ©Laurian Taler, 2004

A1
The weather is and sometimes isn't as you wish
The seasons are as slippery as is a fish
The days and nights are running wild
Through all the year
And all the years are just unstoppable as you are
My fresh morning

A2
The hours go and minutes pass without a tick
Only the seconds come to make me feel so sick
It is the love sick that I go through from the time
I cannot see you till I see you once again
My fresh morning

B1
A spring with sun and clouds and storms
You come, tempestuous, in my life
With you, the moon grows ocean's tides
And winter backs away its strife.

B2
A spring, with clouds and storms and sun
Forever you make life so green
To you, with happy eyes I run
To keep you 'n my arms I am keen.

Chorus
Pom -porom porom porom po- pom
Pom -porom porom porom po- pom
Pom -porom porom porom po- pom
Pom -porom porom porom po- pom
Pom

07 02. **It Happened**

Music & lyrics ©Laurian Taler, 2006

A
It happened when I did not know
That it would come
A tremor and a doubt, a heart beat
And then some
A furtive glance, an accidental stroke
And smile
An obsession, a desire
To hold you 'n my arms

B
From there on things went
As far as they could go
A marriage and a life
With ups and downs, you know,
Then separation, 'cause
We couldn't stand ourselves
And then a divorce to part
For a new, luckier start

07 03. **We Go**
Music & lyrics ©Laurian Taler, 2004

A1
We go, we go. / Where we go,
We fly, we fly / High in the sky,
We crawl, we run / Toward the sun
On a beam / Of a dream

A2
We feel, we deal / For soul and meal,
We laugh, we cry, / We don't know why,
We look for truth / Ruthless or smooth
And we find / Our kind

B
Why am I a fool,
Why are you a fool,
Why aren't we so sage
To love beyond age
Wherever are you
I am there too
Kneading souls together
In happiness
Wherever are you
I am there too
Kneading souls together
In happiness
Why am I a fool,
Why are you a fool,
Why aren't we so sage
To love beyond age.

07 04. **Dance Me**
Music & lyrics © Laurian Taler, 2002

A1

Dance me
I urge you dance me
The way you always
Have done
Dance me
I like this tune now
You know how we can
Have fun

B (2x)

Dance me
I want to feel admired
Dance me
My body is all fired
Dance me
I think I feel inspired
By you
And this song

A2

Dance me
With passion dance me
Make me a part
Of your beat
Dance me
Forever dance me
It's where
Our souls meet

B (2x)

C (2x)

 While you dance
You are so much
A tempest
While you dance
You give to life
So much zest
While you dance
The world turns fast
Around you
It's love's chance
You take just
While you dance.

A1, B

07 05. **Relax**
Music & lyrics ©Laurian Taler, 2007

A
It's time to relax and smell the flowers
It's time to relax and smile inside
It's time to relax and take the showers
With a grain of salt and wisdom to embrace
It is time to watch the sunset colours
It is time to see the shooting stars
It's time to relax and smell the flowers
It's time to relax and smile inside

B
Time to relax now
Time to relax now
Time to relax now
Time to relax now
Time to relax now
Time to relax now
Time to relax now
You must do just that

A, B

07 06. **What Do You Know**
Music and lyrics ©Laurian Taler, 2004

A1
What do you know
Of the void that I own
What do you know
How I feel when alone
What do you know
Of my searching in vain
       Of the stars, of the rain

A2
What do you know
Of my trembling inside
What do you know
Where I'm looking for guide
What do you know
Where I'm trying to go
       Through the fog, through the snow

B
You just caress me as only you know
You just address me with words that can glow
You just get lost looking deep in my eyes
You love entice

A3
What do you know
Of the links in my chains
What do you know
Of the blocks in my brains
What do you know
Of the choices I missed
       In the light, in the mist

B

To hold out I don't know (3x)

07 07. <u>**There Isn't Another Way**</u>
Music & lyrics ©Laurian Taler, 2004

Intro:

If there is another way of dealing
With the many problems of mankind
Come and tell me if you are most willing
To fight for them with your soul and mind

A1
Sing with courage
There isn't another way
To be you
Paint with flowers
There isn't another way
To be true
Play with abandon
There isn't another way
To enjoy

B
Life is just a bit of dust
Filled with spark
Under a crust
Light the fire
Share your light
Happiness will be
In your sight

Ending:

Live with courage my fellow
With courage my fellow
There isn't another way

07 08. **<u>Tell Me What</u>**
Music & lyrics ©2005 Laurian Taler

A1
Tell me what's on your mind
What deep resentments do you grind
Just make me understand
This love how can we again mend

A2
Say what you have to say
Whatever is, I'll try to cope
Just do not go away
Clear my thoughts and give me hope
Just do not go away
Clear my thoughts and give me hope

B
Every time I think of you, my love, I tremble,
Goose bumps suddenly grow on my skin, I scramble,
My throat narrows thin, and all my feelings start
 'Cause you are my queen, you are my queen
My throat narrows thin, and all my feelings start
 'Cause you are my queen, indeed you are my queen

07 09. **Funny Harmonica**
Music & lyrics ©Laurian Taler, 2004

A1
My head is full of my harmonica
Of sounds that cry and put me into mood
It begs, it shouts, it prays as much as could
My little mouth harmonica

A2
It's funny how I got attached to it
This little thing that doesn't miss a beat
It follows me and sure I follow her
My little mouth harmonica

Chorus
Blow my soul into the vibrant space
Bring another soul or heart to race
Make the air tremble hard with you
Give me peace as only you can do

A3
When I am sad I start to play the thing
When I am happy it might make me swing
And when I want to make you understand
It works as hard as one full band

A4
Funny harmonica, you make me proud
Even if you are never much too loud
Even if your sound travels just so far
Funny harmonica you are

Chorus (2x)

07 10.   **Remember, Remember**
Music & lyrics ©Laurian Taler, 2001

A1
Remember, remember
Our last fight
Remember, remember
We cried all night
Remember, remember
T'was no one's fault
Both knew we wanted just love
(But we didn't know
 That love has its own price)

A2
Remember, remember
Our love has grown
Remember, remember
We're no more alone
Remember, remember
Our fruit of love
Asks us to care for it
(Children need their parents
To care for them)

B
Look at our child
(S)he is the apple of my eye
Look at our child
(S)he is the apple of your eye
I see in him (her)
All the hope love has brought us
You see in him (her)
Past, present and beyond

C (2x)
Give me your hand
Love me again
Give me your heart
Love me again
Give me your love
Love me again
Love me again
Forever

07 11. **A Dreamer**
Music and lyrics ©Laurian Taler, 2004

A
A dreamer I was born
And a dreamer I will stay
Till my midnight
My soul is filled with dreams
And my eyes are seeing things
Closed or open

B
Tortured by life
Escape in night
Without borders
Without orders
I am just what I dream
And I dream of seraphim
That I'll make with you
Tonight.

C
No matter how hard it will be
I'll make this dream alive, you'll see,
We'll build our future,
We'll build our future,
We'll start our future
Tonight
(bis)

08 01. **A Rotten Day**
Music & lyrics ©Laurian Taler, 2005

A1
A rotten day I have
And don't you ask me why
A rotten day I have
I yawn and then I sigh
Whatever I intend
It goes out off my hand
And when I try to think
I can't find any link

B
Rotten day - get off!
And rotten night -get off!
Oh rotten day- leave me now
And rotten night- I don't know how

C
I need to be just what I want
I need to be a master of my own
I need to be just what I want
I need to be a master of my own conception
I need to learn
I need to earn
Respect of my deep self
I need to plan
To be a man
I need to ban
Bad thoughts that linger in mind
And start again

A2
A rotten day I had
But I feel better now
Nobody makes me mad
I'll start to plan ahead
Good humour, many hopes
And step by step I'll go
(3x)
'Cause whatever I want
I'll catch it in my ropes

08 02. **From A Heart**
Music & lyrics ©Laurian Taler, 2005

Instrumental A, B

A1
 From a heart to another
All my best feelings flow
Trying to offer
 What's in my soul

B1
Never did I think
That love is
Just a game with boys and girls
Never did I think that love is
Just a game with boys and girls

 Instrumental A, B

A2
You played with my feelings
As with a set of cards
Bluffing so lovely
All thousand yards

B2
Never did you think that love is
More than a game to bluff and win
Never did you think that love is
More than a game to bluff and win

08 03. **<u>Last Encounter</u>**
Music & lyrics ©Laurian Taler, 2005

A
Remember what
You said
Remember what
You said

Remember what you said
At our last encounter
I thought that every word
 Comes truly from your heart
But now I see that you
Have done the same as others
Whose words are worth the same,
They cheat and then they maim

B
You said that love
Will ever be
Between us
And that we will share
Ourselves for all our life
That we will grow old together
And discover all the bliss in our souls.

A

08 04. **Melancholy / Blue Nostalgy**
Music & lyrics ©Laurian Taler, 2005

A1
Blue nostalgy, disrobe me of your veil,
Blue nostalgy, blow wind away your sail,
I want to run from you,
I want to hide from you,
But you keep always closer to my tail.

I want to run from you,
I want to hide from you,
But you keep always closer to my tail.

A2
Melancholy, you beat me at my game
Melancholy, my soul's core why you maim,
I want to run from you,
I want to hide from you,
But you are on my case just all the same.

I want to run from you,
I want to hide from you,
But you are on my case just all the same.

B1
From now whatever sadness will come to me
From now whatever sadness around I'll see
I'll make it vanish like a ghost
And of my life I'll make the most
And of my life I'll truly make the most.

I'll make it vanish like a ghost
And of my life I'll make the most
And of my life I'll truly make the most.

08 05. **<u>Moves Of Passion</u>**
Music & lyrics ©Laurian Taler, 2005

A
You have told me "come"
You'll be learning some
Of the moves of passion
You need just a session
Of the tango dance
I have gone with you
And after a few
Of your strong embraces
I changed many faces
And fell into a trance

B
Now I dance with you
Now I feel with you
And have become romantic
Keeping you 'n my arms
Possessed by your charms
I become so frantic
You are elegant
Body undulant
You put me on fire
Life is only you
Love is only you
When we dance tango.

08 06. **Into Hot Water**
Music & lyrics ©Laurian Taler, 2005

A1
I ' ve got into hot water
I don't know what to do
My girl saw me last morning
With someone that's called Sue

A2
It's not it was just morning
I was with Sue in bed
And when my lover came in
She instantly turned red
B1
I told you I 'm in trouble
I don't know how to cope
She'd throw me out to rubble
Without soap
B2
I told you I 'm in trouble
I don't know how to cope
I told you I 'm in trouble
I don't know how to cope
I'm in hot water
I'm in so hot water!
C
I want no more nor Sue and no other
I promise I won't be any bother
I'll be a saint, a monk and no pain
Just get me back again
Just get me back again, my darling
I want no more nor Sue and no other
Just get me back again

A1, A2, B1

08 07. **Share - Share**
Music & lyrics ©Laurian Taler, 2005

A1
Share, share
If you care
What's on earth
And what's in air

A2
Share, share
 Or you dare
Make the planet
Become bare

A3
Share, share
You are fair
We can't live
If food turns (for all) so rare

A4
Share, share
Don't just stare
World is grim
If you ain 't there

B (2x)
Be one for all
Act for our goal
Save mankind's planet
All for one and always one for all

08 08. **Slow Road**
Music & lyrics ©Laurian Taler, 2005

A1
Slow highway, slow road I see ahead
As gentle as power allows
Slow highway, slow road I see ahead
Life lets you run only so much

A2
Slow highway, slow road I see ahead
My love is as always, with me
With many years under our belts
We are hoping to walk us in wisdom

B
Whatever hardship may come when we reach our trials
It's good to know that we 'll be as were ever together
And with good friends and our loved ones with us
We hope that all hurdles we will pass

A3
So into slow road we just go
Blue sky or grey sky or some foe
We are serene as our deeds all have been
Wishing peace to people and all goodness with keen

A1, A2

08 09. **<u>When Coming Through The Crowd</u>**
Music & lyrics ©Laurian Taler, 2005

A
When coming through the crowd
I saw two burning eyes
That pierced me
And when they disappeared
Behind the moving crowd
My heart shrank
B
I frantically tried
To find again those eyes
And swimming through the crowd
 I got another glimpse
But after such a bliss
I lost that look again
For a while.

A, B

C
Those burning eyes have followed
My shadow of a man
Those burning eyes have hollowed
Whatever I began

But when they reappeared
My spirit has returned
I married eyes of lover
And for them still
I lovingly yearn

08 10. **The Tale Of Tristan And Isolde**
Music and lyrics ©Laurian Taler, 2006

A1
The tale of Tristan and Isolde
For so many centuries is told
It makes you believe that a mate
You may find according to fate
3x
But as destiny turns against you
You must find a way out of the blue

B
In the darkest of despairs
If you have a star as light
And this star you know that cares
You may overcome in fight

A2
Tristan killed in fight the betrothed
That Isolde hoped to unclothed
A poisoned Tristan found a haven
With Isolde and with her maven
3x
But as destiny turns against you
You must find a way out of the blue

A3
Tristan won Isolde for his king
Although they both fell into loving
She married the king but loved Tristan
Who died loving her non-resistant
3x
But as destiny turns against you
You must find a way out of the blue

09 01. **Rega, Rega, Reggae**
Music & lyrics ©Laurian Taler, 2008

A
Rega. rega, reggae
Wait a moment reggae
I have so much, darling
On my soul

 Rega. rega, reggae,
Wait a moment reggae,
I can carry only
One full bowl

 Rega, rega, reggae,
Wait a moment reggae,
Let me breath more deeply
For a while

Otherwise I'm cracking
Otherwise I'm bursting,
Otherwise I'm grooving
Till I'm breaking down

B (2X)
Take it easy, take it easy,
Give me time
Take it easy, take it easy,
Keep me prime

09 02. **Trick Me No More**
Music and lyrics ©Laurian Taler, 2000

No, you'll trick me no more
You will trick me no more
Nothing my heart will feel
Will be no sore

You will trick me no more
You will trick me no more
My heart will nothing feel
Will be no sore

I have waited for so long
I can wait no more so long
I won't long for you no more
No more, oh, no more

I'll go out and find a man
Who will care, so I can
Say my heart is not in pain
No more, oh, no more

09 03. **<u>Angry Souls</u>**
Music & lyrics ©Laurian Taler, 2006

A1
Angry souls should count to twenty
Angry souls should learn to swear
Angry souls should flex their muscles
Angry souls should know to bear

A2
Angry souls should value silence
'Cause silence is said to be always golden
Angry souls should value reason
And the feelings of the world

B (2x)
Sun doesn't set
On your regret
Anger 's short madness
That will punish
Somebody for null
Don't be an angry soul
Be in control
Water your fire
Life is always waiting
For your role

09 04. **<u>Snowgrass</u>**
Music & lyrics ©Laurian Taler, 2007, 2011

A1
Snowgrass makes me think of you
Thin, green, and so tough to handle
On the mountains of my youth
Seeking a higher truth

A2
Snowgrass brings back memories
Of the time that we were younger
When we went to change the world
And in the grass we curled

B
Our sky was bluer
The horizon larger
The valleys were deeper
Our eyes brighter
And we flew high farther
Wings of desire
That flapped as our hearts
Sang the beauty surrounding us

Our sky was bluer
The horizon larger
The valleys were deeper
Our eyes brighter
And we flew high farther
Wings of desire
That flapped as our hearts
Sang the beauty surrounding our love

A1, A2, B

09 05. <u>**We Are Burning Rubber**</u>
Music & lyrics ©Laurian Taler, 2007

AE
We are burning rubber and are burning gas,
'Cause we love around us to create a perfect mess
We go up the mountains and we leave our trash
We pollute the air as we are ever so brash

BE
We, the generation that says ALL FOR ME,
And who doesn't care what future will be
We who want huge houses and drive monster cars
For us there's no limit,
For us life's a farce
We will stop at nothing to have fun

AF
Nous brûlons l'elastique et brûlons le gaz,
 Parce que nous aimons autour créer un chock parfait
 Nous montons montagnes ou laissons débris
 Nous polluons tout l'air
Car nous sommes jamais si crasses

BF
Nous, la troupe qui indique TOUS POUR MOI,
 Et qui s'inquiète pas quel futur sera
Nous qui voulons des voitures énormes
 Pour nous pas d'limite,
 Dans la farce de la vie
Nous nous arrêterons à rien

09 06. <u>**Try A Song**</u>
Music & lyrics ©Laurian Taler, 2002,2005

A
Try a song
Sing a song
Nothing makes you
Happier
Dance a song
Mime a song
Act a song
For better time

B
With just seven notes
You change your spleen
With just seven notes
You come out clean
Music brings enjoyment
To your heart
And it makes you happier
To play your part.

09 07. **What You Own**

Music and lyrics ©Laurian Taler, 2005

A1
What you own is not important
If you share with a smile
All the treasures of your feelings
With the people that you mind
A2
What you own is not important
If the earth and sun and sky
Are the borders of your laughter
And you meet them saying Hi

B
Gold and precious stones
Land, whoever owns
Real love will not buy
Friendship with all kind
And Peace for mankind
Makes us happy and good
But when some are so much
Into owning stuff
Many are left with just nothing
Or enough to get starved

A3
What you own is not important
If you share with a smile
All the treasures of your feelings
With the people that you mind

A4
Share wisdom, share knowledge
And break bread with all the ones
Who are helping make this planet
Liveable for everyone

09 08. **<u>Good Day</u>**
Music & lyrics ©Laurian Taler, 2000

A
Good day to you
Tiny princess Pearl
You make my day
If you smile or curl
You 're my silent sea
You're my bluest sky
Hope and happiness
You bring high
B1
Days full of smiles
Full of meaning
And love
Nights full of hopes
Full of worries
And love
Months and then years
Watching you growing up
Storm full of life
Full of love
B2
What will you be
Just be good
To mankind
What will you be
Just be tender
And kind
What will you be
Will spring love
In my heart
Storm full of life
Full of love

09 09. **<u>You Gush Fascination</u>**
Music & lyrics ©Laurian Taler, 2005

A
You gush fascination
From whatever you
Do or show or wear
You gush fascination
From whatever you
Say or sing or dare

B
I am smitten by your soul
Captivated by your splendour
You are opening the door
To my limitless surrender

09 10. **What Inspiration Gives You**
Music & lyrics ©Laurian Taler, 2005

A1
What inspiration gives you
Of it one tries one's best
'Cause only so is spreading
And it becomes a fest

A2
I don't know what the words are
To speak of harmony
But this is what my music
Would try for you to be

A3
It can be without loudness
And too much ho and hum
It wants your heart to warm up
 Not break your ear drum

B
Another song for another soul
It is supposed to heal and make
Infinity more bearable
And darkness held again at bay.

A1, B, A2

10 01. **<u>At The Fest</u>**

(Country ballad)
Music & lyrics ©Laurian Taler, 2005

A1
At the fest, when I went
I was lonely and meant
That I'll find for myself a good bride
I just couldn't believe
Such a feat I'll achieve
And I 'll turn to my room as a groom

A2
But when you raised your eyes
Your smile was paradise
And my heart warmed like never before
I decided I 'll dive
To keep this love alive
'Cause it's you that I so much adore

B1
With two bottles and a tray of bratwurst
I made my attempt to get you closer
But it wasn't easy to approach you
As you kept running to see your friends

A1 A2

B2
As I tried to close in to your party
I tripped and I stretched long like a barn broom
But you pulled me up and smiled like heaven
And it's so that I became your groom

A3

At the fest, as I guessed
I found myself a bride
Who has always a smile
On her face
She 's devoted to me
And she's fast as a bee
'Cause it's good
When you marry an ace

A4
We'll have a bunch of kids
Who will learn all the creeds
Of the life on a free open space
And when grown strong and good
We will take them to feasts
Each of them to encounter their ace

10 02. **Joy Bossa Nova**
Music & lyrics © Laurian Taler, 2001

A (2x)
Dance bossa nova
Sing bossa nova
Play bossa nova
For your joy
Beat bossa nova
Hum bossa nova
Chant bossa nova
For your joy

B
Dancing bossa nova
Eyes start a-glowing
And with them burns
My heart just for you
Dancing bossa nova
Hearts come together
Minds come together
To feel a-new

C (2x)
Bursting of temptation
Full of desire
Feel the palpitation
We are on fire
Waving with the beat
We wallow in wonder
And become so fonder
Of our joy

10 03. **Man Went Out Of Jail**
Music and words ©Laurian Taler, 2004

Man went out of jail
And troubled,
Wanted to kill wife,
Shot her but he missed
And troubled,
Hit her with his gun,
As he had to flee from there,
Cops in his pursuit,
He took bystander as hostage
Gun ready to shoot.

With one arm he choked the woman
Gun aimed to her head
Right in front of Union Station
Neither sane nor mad.

As cops kept him surrounded
And asked to let her go
Crowds watched the scene bewildered
As if at a show
Big man holding girl hostage
Gun aimed to her head
It was just like in the movies
But real and bad.

Then a bullet from a shooter
Hit his head
Then a bullet from a shooter
Hit his head
Then a bullet from a shooter
Hit his head
Then a bullet from a shooter
Hit his head
And the big man,
Suicidal,
Fell dead.
That's the story of a passion gone
Badly mad.

10 05 **Only Trouble**
Music & lyrics ©2004 Laurian Taler

Intro

What do I do with you
What can I do with you
When I just close my eyes
You jump and torture again my soul

A
You breath only trouble
You provoke to sin
You turned me a rubble
Out of flesh and skin
You are hot and icy
And you make me burn
You are much too spicy
Now I learn

B
Let me go, let me go
Free my mind, free my mind
Be so kind, be so kind
Free my mind, free my mind
Stay away, stay away
From my dreams, from my dreams
Stay away, stay away
Don't send flames, don't send flames
In my soul

Final

What do I do with you
What can I do with you
When I just close my eyes
You jump and torture again my soul

10 06 **Remember What You Said**
Music & lyrics ©Laurian Taler, 2005

A

Remember what
You said
Remember what
You said

Remember what you said
At our last encounter
I thought that every word
Comes truly from your heart
But now I see that you
Have done the same as others
Whose words are worth the same?
They cheat and then they maim

B
You said that love
Will ever be
Between us
And that we will share
Ourselves for all our life
That we will grow old together
And discover all the bliss in our souls.

10 07 **Sing When Sun**
Music & lyrics ©Laurian Taler, 2005

A1,
Sing, when everything around you is like spring
Sing, when sun and moon, and stars are all in concert
Sing, with all your heart and all your soul you sing
What is your call for happiness

A2
Sing, when everything around you 's summery
Sing, when children have in eyes the spark of heaven
Sing, when flowers and when trees are in their green
Showing with pride their beauty

A3 instrumental

B
Life can be so full, so full of laments
Life can be so full of grumble and groans
It's better to change approach
Get yourself a singing coach
And approach life with a livelier song

A1 (2X)
What 's your call for happiness
What 's your call for happiness

10 08 **<u>Songs Are To Sing</u>**
Music & lyrics ©Laurian Taler, 2005

A
Songs are to sing
What is the beauty in our life
Songs are to sing
What do we feel

Songs are to sing
Where your eyes shine with love
Songs are to sing
How you can smile

Songs are my friends
When I am low and I'm sad
Songs make my heart
Pound with the rhythm

Songs bring the hope
That you will all move like one
Songs pair with you
To make things done.

B

If I cannot sing, I hurt
If I cannot sing, I hurt
Life seems not much more than dirt
Life seems not much more than dirt
(CODA BIS)
If I cannot sing, I hurt
So much.

10 09 **<u>School Starts In Autumn</u>**
Music & lyrics ©Laurian Taler, 2008

A
School starts in autumn
School starts in autumn
I'm so excited
That I can't explain
Meeting new people
And learning a fortune
And rubbing a frenzy of thoughts

B
I decided that my road in life
Goes through knowing what I need to know
To be able to build what I want
Make a marking future for all my world

C1
I 'll learn how to grow most flowers
I'll learn where to find energy
I'll design
What never was
I'll invent
Better worlds

 C2
I 'll learn how to deal with brethren
I'll learn how to juggle heavy tasks
I'll spread love
That will well thrive
I'll stir up
Sanity
I'll stir up
Sanity

10 10   The Meek Inherit The Earth

Music & lyrics ©Laurian Taler, 2005

A
The meek inherit the earth
They save it from certain death
With care and with so much love
Forests they plant, and work the soil

B
The meek inherit the earth
They save it from certain death
With care and so much love
With their brains and with their toil

C
You have the brains and the power
You must do what's in your power
You have the brains and the power
You must do what's in your power

A, B

D
Do your part, do your part
And save the earth
Do your part, do your part
And save the earth

Album titles (CDs) in this collection of songs:

01 Fair Game
02 Forbidden Fiesta
03 Kiss Me Gently
04 Simple Love
05 Wonder
06 Have Hope
07 Funny Harmonica
08 A Rotten Day
09 Try A Song
10 Only Trouble

Album titles (CDs) in other collections of songs:

11 You Gush Fascination
12 One Earth – The Musical
13 You Know Me
14 Don't Pray for Me
15 Listen To Your Heart
16 All This Jazz
17 Dancing Slowly
18 Don't Fly Alone
19 A Train Left Late
20 Always A Flower
21 On A Blade
22 We Have Had So Many Days
23 Summer
24 Build Me A Map
25 Zazie Rumba
26 Do Not Rush Love
27 Passion Runs Me

Some of these albums can be found on the author's website, www.gongnog.com

A special CD with all the songs in this volume is available in mp3 format. You may order it from www.gongnog.com.

Look for the other volumes of lyrics in the series "Songs of Love and Mores", named "On a blade of grass" and "Under the blue sky", to be published soon.

N.B. - The songs on pages 92 and 115 are the same, albeit with different titles. The repetition is due to being placed in different albums.

ALMOST ESSENTIALS
Lyrics from my songs

ALL RIGHTS RESERVED
GONG PUBLISHING TORONTO
www.gongnog.com

ISBN 978-1-926477-00-8

www.ingramcontent.com/pod-product-compliance
Lightning Source LLC
Chambersburg PA
CBHW060404090426
42734CB00011B/2259